NO!
Not My Son!

An African Mother's
Journey Through
Life with Autism

DR. TADE AKERE

Paperback ISBN - 978-1-7371861-2-0

Published by Dewalette Creations LLC

Printed in the United States of America

NO!

Not My Son!

*An African Mother's
Journey Through
Life with Autism*

DR. TADE AKERE

Contents

Introduction

"Your son has Autism."

The words hit me like a lighting bolt and I thought, "Autism? What is that? Surely, it can be fixed. I just have to find out the cause and then I can find a cure." It was that simple. I have conquered worse, how hard could this possibly be? I had a plan and that was to make him talk. "If I could just get him to communicate," I thought, "all will be well". Determined to overcome this minor hurdle that had come my way, I went to the local library and checked out all the books I could find on Autism. I went home, then went straight to work. "I will find a cure, I will beat this!" I continued to say to myself.

As I did my research, with each book I read, the more the reality struck me that this was a lifelong disability. A lifelong disability? There is no way my son will grow up not being able to communicate. I could not even imagine it. The panic gripped my heart. My heart raced as I felt the fear grip me. My chest tightened as I thought of how my son would get through life not being able to communicate.

How would he get through life? I cried, "NO! NOT MY SON! WHY MY SON?" And the Lord replied, "WHY NOT YOUR SON? Whose son should it be? Who in your opinion is more deserving? It is not because you or your husband has sinned, but that My name may be glorified."

I started to write this book years ago and could not bring myself to complete it. The reason is simple; the story is still unfolding and I don't know if this book will ever be completed. I say this because my experience is a journey–a life-long journey, a journey that ends the day we leave this world. You see, I am a living testimony of the mercies of God and there are new experiences to add on every day. I feel like my life is being upgraded with the breaking of each new dawn.

My son, Yinka, is 23 years old now, and he aged out of the school system the day he turned 22 (December 25th, 2019). He continues to make great strides both academically and in the arts. He played the trombone in his middle school concert band and he did the same in high school. He plays the piano beautifully and he loves to read books and listen to music. Nineteen years ago, I was told to take him home and not bother to waste any resources on him because he will never be able to speak or engage in meaningful conversations or activities like his peers.

I wish I could remember the name of the speech pathologist that dismissed my request for a referral for speech services with that statement. I remember as I sat in her office watching a group of students interact with him. He did not make eye contact or respond to their questions or requests. This led them to conclude that he was mentally retarded and that he would never be able to talk. The conclusion of the visit was a recommendation to take my son home and make the best of a bad situation. I left the doctor's office crushed and disappointed. I drove home thinking, "There has got to be another way". I was determined not to give up. I knew my son and I saw the potential in him. I refused to be defeated by this monster called Autism.

> *I was determined not to give up. I knew my son and I saw the potential in him. I refused to be defeated by this monster called Autism.*

Since my son was five, I was advised to put him on a waiting list for a group home.

Since I started this book over a decade ago, it is fair to note that there have been huge strides made in the response and intervention of autism, in terms of creating awareness, diagnosing and treating it. My story spans two continents and I can safely say that since the book began, there has also been increased awareness in the two continents.

Even though the African Continent may not yet be on the forefront of diagnosis and intervention, I am proud to say that there has been increased awareness over the years.

1: Different Worlds

I am the parent of a child with unique challenges, and I live in two worlds that view individuals with challenges in very different ways. Parenting a child with unique challenges while being strongly influenced by two different cultures has completely altered my worldview, taking me to the utmost in human endurance. This journey has developed me in ways of thinking that were surprising to me. It has been a unique journey of struggle in living and being.

Where I am today in my own knowledge and understanding of what it means to be the parent of a child with unique challenges is far from the quiet and safe neighborhood where I originally started this journey in Lagos, Nigeria. There were many times when I wanted to give up this struggle but the Higher Being that lives within me, God Almighty, always had His wind beneath my wings. I often find comfort in the book of Isaiah 40:31 which reads, "*But those who wait on the Lord shall renew their strength; they shall mount up with wings like eagles, they shall run and not be weary,*

They shall walk and not faint.". Each time I grew faint and weary and felt I could not go any further, God always had a

> *God always had a way of giving me new strength for each new day.*

way of giving me new strength for each new day. It is to Him that I give all the glory because I know that if it had not been the Lord on my side I would have been consumed. Consumed by the sheer magnitude of the situation; consumed by the unexpected coldness and callousness from the world around; consumed by the absence of much needed support - consciously and other times out of fear, ignorance or just a lack of knowing how to give support.

I have been exposed to two continents that approach autism or any disability with diametrically opposite reactions. The truth is that, until recent years, autism has been an enigma and still remains such to a large population across the globe. These two worlds treat children with special challenges quite differently. Sub-Saharan Africa views the special needs child with suspicious indifference but the Western world views the child with hopeful intervention. In the course of writing this book, I have grown tremendously and I have learned that sometimes suspicious indifference could be a result of fear of the unknown. As human beings we generally tend to fear what we do not know and we treat the unexplainable with suspicion. For indigenes of the African continent and those in the diaspora, there is a biblical saying hedged in our thinking, "A curse causeless does not alight." In other words, there is a reason why people go through trials. The average African believes you must have done something to bring misfortune upon yourself. Another school of thought in that same environment might interpret it slightly differently and say that someone has put a curse on you and that has caused you to have a child with a disability. They say things like: *This is not normal, this is spiritual; you are being punished for your sins. Maybe if you pray hard enough, God will have mercy on you and heal your son. You must be engaged in some great sin for God to choose to punish you this way. Whoever you offended must be really mad at you.* For the most part, this world has very little understanding of this situation and the best way to deal with it is to act like it is not there. These children are seen as an embarrassment to the family and society at large. They are therefore not quite exposed to the larger society for fear of the stigma it will bring on the family. A number of these children who are born into wealthy families are sent abroad by their parents and kept in private facilities where they can be better managed and more so kept away from the public eyes and wagging tongues of friends and family members.

The western world as I mentioned earlier views disabilities with hopeful intervention.

Although I must admit that in the western society, there are still those who have zero tolerance for children with disabilities and also feel that these children are not worth the amount of time and the money spent on their education by the government, the insurance companies and the parents. They would rather spend the money on sports and scholarships for typical growing children if the end result will put their school on the map of success and open doors for more grants and scholarships.

While the opposition in one part of the world may be social, the opposition from the other world comes from a purely economic standpoint. For one world, it is all about looking good and saving face, while in the other world, it is about the bottom line. Studies show that it costs much more to educate a child with special needs throughout his/her lifetime than it costs to educate a typical growing child. Children with special needs require more resources to be educated. For them to access the curriculum, a team needs to be put in place - Speech therapist, Individual aide, Occupational therapist, Physical therapist, School Psychologist, Counselor and Physician. So much more resources have to be put in place to help the child have a fair shot at being educated.

Research has shown that early intervention is the most effective treatment approach for children with autism.

Studies and reports have shown that children who are exposed to therapy in the first three years of life, tend to do better than their contemporaries who are introduced later.

Autism generally manifests around eighteen months of age and it has been reported by parents of children who start intervention by the age of two or three that the children make tremendous progress or are completely mainstreamed within the school system by the age of five.

In spite of the challenges faced in the African continent, we see that the battles are different. In a society where we are struggling to accept the fact and nature of the disease, it would be difficult to move to the next level which is diagnosis and treatment. You have to first accept that there is a problem and then you ask for help by demanding

As long as parents remain in denial, the journey becomes longer and success becomes bleaker as the child grows older.

and advocating for resources. Then and only then can your children begin the long road to recovery. But as long as parents remain in denial, the journey becomes longer and success becomes bleaker as the child grows older.

The latter world is the one which I have gratefully found myself in. My husband and I migrated to the United States in 1992 and 1993 respectively. My husband (then fiancee) came first in 1992. We had met and fallen in love fresh out of college. We met at the National Youth Service Corps (NYSC) camp in Ipaja, Lagos and fate brought us together again when I was posted to the United Bank for Africa (UBA), where he happened to be a customer. We started seeing each other regularly and we spent most of our time talking about our hopes and dreams. We had mutual dreams of moving to the United States. The plan was that he would continue his medical career, I would get an MBA, we would have 3 kids and we would live happily ever after. It sounds like a fairytale life and that is what we did. We settled down to life in the US and God showed us favor.

Our early years in the U.S. involved working jobs in Walgreens, Strawberry (a shoe store in New York city), a $10 clothing store in Manhattan. This particular job remains an amusement to me. It was owned by a family from Turkey. The store had rolling ladders up to the ceiling. The clothes were stored all the way up and whenever a customer needed a particular color or size, the sales girls would climb up the ladder and get them what they wanted. I remember dreaming of owning the same type of clothes that were sold at the store because I could not afford them at the time. After a year in New York, we moved to Chicago to be closer to my husband's family. We had come to visit for Christmas after my dad had passed away suddenly in Nigeria and I was unable to travel home. I was devastated and inconsolable. We decided to visit his brother in Chicago and I fell in love with the beautiful, laid back city that was a far cry from my home town Lagos and New York city.

Chicago was a breath of fresh air. For the first time, I felt I was in the real America. My husband got a job as a parking lot attendant; he drove a Taxi cab and delivered newspapers. I worked at Walgreens and Carson Pierre Scott. After studying and taking his USMLE exams, my husband got into residency at the well renowned Cook County Hospital (now John H. Stroger Hospital) on the west-side hospital district of Chicago. I eventually got a job with Citibank and life was good. We had decided to wait before having children but the pressures from family members grew.

We started the process of getting pregnant but it was not happening. We decided to visit a doctor to determine why I was not getting pregnant. The truth is that I was not getting a period which meant I was not ovulating and I was perfectly fine with that until I realized that I could not get pregnant without having a menstrual cycle. We were declared an infertile couple by a fertility specialist. The truth was that as a teenager I had painful periods. Every month was dreaded as I would be knocked down with severe dysmenorrhea for the first two days of my period. Eventually, I stopped having a period and there were times when I would not get a period for six to nine months.

As a young woman, I was glad not having to go through

the excruciating five days of pain. As we got into the second year of marriage, our parents started getting impatient for a grandchild. In spite of the fact that we had decided to wait until we were financially and mentally ready, we caught the impatience bug and started to try but nothing was happening. The first issue was to get me to have a period so I could ovulate and get pregnant but it was not that easy. I was prescribed pills that made me ovulate and pills to make me menstruate but still no pregnancy. By now we had been in the US for four years and had no kids.

After the doctor referred us to another fertility specialist, we got pregnant without any warning. The pregnancy was so unexpected but we were overjoyed. My oldest son Ayodeji Michael was born nine months later and he brought us so much joy as he still does today. My mother was recently retired at the time, so she was overjoyed to drop everything and came to help us with her first grandchild. We had it so easy with grandma's help that we did not realize that we were pregnant again until I was almost 4 months pregnant. I had a newborn barely 5 months and we had another baby on the way. We concluded that God wanted to reward us for the years we waited so we were elated at the idea of another baby although we would have preferred to wait at least two years to have another one.

Ayoyinka Immanuel was born on a cold Christmas morning with no complications. After he was born, the Doctor told us that he needed a blood transfusion due to an infection I had during the pregnancy. We refused the transfusion and that was it. We took our new baby home and we settled into parenthood as we knew it. What more could we want? We had 2 beautiful, healthy baby boys and life was good.

We visited the pediatrician for Yinka's eighteen month visit and the doctor asked us how many words he could say. We responded with about 7 words that he constantly echoed but there were no spontaneous words. She referred us to the early intervention program in our school district and that was the beginning of my life as I know it today.

In spite of the constant battles with the school districts about providing much needed services for my son, I always thank my God that my son was born on the other side of the Atlantic ocean. Here there are services and resources available to be fought for as opposed to a society that is still struggling to accept that an epidemic (worse than AIDS or cancer, in my opinion) has quietly crept into our homes and is stealing the minds of our children and the joy and peace of many parents.

I had my son in my thirties and until I had him, I had never heard the word Autism. Today, I can say that the average Nigerian has either never heard that word and or does not have a full understanding of the disease. Once we got the diagnosis, we were loaded with resources that helped us get the ball rolling. I often wonder what would have become of my son if he had not been born in this part of the world.

In the other world, majority of children with disabilities like my son are kept indoors for the most part. Their parents are ashamed to bring them out in public because it is seen as a curse in that part of the world. Most of these children are denied the much needed education and social interaction, mostly because there are not enough resources available and most teachers in the schools are not trained to teach children with special needs. Hence, you will find the average special child at home doing nothing and with no hope for the future. If the parents are fortunately wealthy, they will fly these children to boarding schools abroad, but sadly, there are hundreds whose parents cannot afford such luxuries.

Unfortunately, in Africa, you'll find the average special child at home doing nothing and with no hope for the future.

2: My Pain, My Shame

In addition to the role of being a parent of a child with unique challenges, I had peculiar experiences being a female born in a modern African culture, and then settling in a modern American culture. Nothing prepared me for what has become my life story today. Becoming a woman, a wife and then a mother, and now being a parent of this unique child presents a unique challenge to parenting. It makes me a unique parent, and I must tell my story.

Truthfully, I must admit that being a unique parent has been the most unexpected and challenging of all my life's experiences. I know being a unique parent in this modern day Twenty-first century is nothing like being a parent in the "old days", because the conditions are so different.

To be a successful parent today, you must be deliberate about learning how to be successful at raising your children. There is hardly any room to be a successful parent if your knowledge is based

To be a successful parent today, you must be deliberate about learning how to be successful at raising your children.

on "lucky parenting" or traditional ways of parenting. Nowhere in the recorded history of 'human parenting' have the roles and responsibilities of parenting engendered such demands on accuracy in parenting skills. The competition is fierce and there is no room for error. Every parent wants to raise the perfect child, as we are often judged by our parenting skills or lack of it. In most African cultures, your child's behavior is a reflection of who you are and the type of parent that you are. Our parents always told us to "remember the child of whom you are". This meant that we had to behave properly in public and not bring shame and dishonor to the family name.

The external and internal forces that are operating in today's world to influence the behaviors of our children have employed the highest schemes and objects available. Modern computerized communication technology has been successful in capturing the minds and bodies of our children. The mind and body of a child diagnosed with autism is complicated and a parent must use available resources to navigate and understand the biological and physiological maze that weaves deep into the soul of the child.

I have learned that today's parents must be aware of the extreme intricacies of a global education, if they want their children to survive and thrive in the educational system.

Parents can no longer trust the educational system to give their child what they will need in terms of preparedness in order to be selected by society for success. Too many children are programmed for failure and their parents stand helplessly by witnessing their demise, when they should be fighting fiercely for their children. The child's future is dependent upon the success of the parent.

As a mother of a child with unique challenges, I have refused to give up the struggle and the hope that one day my child would no longer be labeled autistic but normal. I have refused to accept this diagnosis because I have witnessed too many miracles for me to settle for anything less! As long as there are living testimonies of Parents and children who have overcome this dreadful disability, I am determined that my story will be the same. I pray that mothers out there will not give up hope even when the doctors and the teachers have given up. You are the only hope that your child has to make it in life. God has given us these children to care for; He chose the strongest women on the earth to bless with these extraordinary children. How the lives of these children are shaped lies solely on us and with the help of God, we can do it.

I pray you will not give up hope even when the doctors and the teachers have given up. You are the only hope that your child has to make it in life.

Remember, God never gives us more than we can handle.

As mothers of special children, we should begin to redefine what the world calls success by determining to reshape the lives of the children and presenting them to the world – not as broken vessels but as the unique human beings that they are. Each of these children have a potential hidden deep within them and it is up to the parents (especially mothers) to reach deep and uncover these abilities. I learned from my child that spoken language is not the only form of communication. The fact that a child is not able to speak does not make him mentally retarded or cognitively delayed. The measure of intelligence in the world today is the use of verbal language and how well one can communicate. As mothers/parents, we have to find other creative ways of enabling our children to communicate with and make sense of the world around them.

Today, there are various resources available to families dealing with such challenges for parents and children – all we need to do is find these resources and take advantage of them. However, the greatest resource, in my opinion, is the networking that stems from the support groups formed by parents around the world. There is nothing more comforting and calming than realizing that someone else shares your pain and understands what you are going through. You are not alone in this world and you can discuss freely with people who will not judge you and are not afraid to give you much needed advice and support.

A common challenge faced by parents with special children is that people around them do not understand the problem. Others do not know what to do to help and many people just ignore them or stay away from them. People are afraid to offer help for fear of rejection but if you are reading this book now and you fall into that category, please let me tell you now that the pain is doubled when a parent is ignored instead of acknowledging and offering help.

> *The pain is doubled when a parent is ignored, instead of acknowledging and offering help.*

3: My Pain, My Passion

What my second son did to my life before he was eight years old is now my life's story. Before going through this life-changing ordeal, no one could have made me believe that a little child could have so much power and influence over the parent's life. I had no idea that such a horrific struggle and an elevated blessing could all come in one bundle – my second son.

This experience was nothing like I had experienced as a child growing up in my native town Lagos, Nigeria. Nigeria is Africa's most populated country with about 200 million people in 2019, which is almost half the size of the population in the United States. Nigeria is unlike the United States which has her population spread out over a land area ten times as big as the land area of Nigeria. Most of Nigeria's people are crowded into urban cities. Today, the overcrowding in Nigeria has reached a crisis stage, especially in the urban cities.

Nigeria is rated the sixth oil producing country in the world with a lot of natural and human resources. With so many resources at her disposal, one would expect Nigeria to be at the forefront of finding a solution to the rising epidemic called autism.

In the urban areas in Nigeria, air and water pollution are major problems and money seems more important than health and education. In my research, I realized there are not a lot of Universities that offer Clinical Psychology and Speech Language Pathology in their curricula. Greed and selfishness are rampant in every aspect of culture. With the rising epidemic of autism and other disabilities, I pray the Nigerian government will wake up and begin to deal with this epidemic that is threatening the future of our nation and the world in general.

In my childhood, parents, grandparents and the extended family were the only power and influence in raising children. Parenting was a lot easier because parents had so much help from the family and community. People would rally around and help raise your child regardless of whether the child was a boy or a girl. We strongly believe that it takes a whole village to raise a child.

However, it was believed that a woman did not even have children until she had a son, even when she already had a girl child. A girl is expected to get married and assume her husband's name but a male child will carry on the family name. To have a son was a special blessing, but if he was handicapped or crippled, it was a curse. For these kinds of children the future was bleak and uncertain.

Children who were difficult to manage, like my son, were handled swiftly, severely, and secretively. Harsh punishment was the treatment for difficult children. When I was seven years old, there was a neighbor's boy about five years of age who didn't speak. The other children in the compound would always pick on him, push him around, and generally treat him very badly. There was also a man who attended our church that was very strange. He was a grown man, but he behaved like a child, and I was afraid of him. I was afraid he would touch me, so I stayed far away from him. I asked my mother, "What is wrong with him?" But, she told me to be quiet and pay attention. Topics like that were never discussed and I believe this deprived people of the knowledge they needed to be compassionate toward this unique group of people. Handicapped or crippled people in Nigeria were frequently looked upon as useless. They were often demonized and considered a real burden on the family. Very few were taken care of by their families. Most were abandoned and left destitute.

Handicapped or crippled people in Nigeria are frequently looked upon as useless.

On a trip to Nigeria in July 2007, I visited with my three children. I decided to take my son to a prayer meeting where there was a crowd of people. To my amazement, a group of young adults spent the whole evening pointing out my son to one another and laughing their heads off at his autistic displays – the usual hand flapping, high pitched echolalia. They amused themselves rather than concentrate on the prayer service. I wondered what I would have done if I were in their position, watching this grown kid acting like a child and totally oblivious to the world around him. I realized they had not been exposed to many people like my child and their reaction was out of ignorance.

When I was in school I knew nothing about handicapped children or special education. All the students in the elementary school that I attended were normal children. The only thing that I remember about us being different from each other was whether one was ugly or pretty. I thought I was ugly until I was about ten years of age. It was my first year in secondary school and the older students were always saying what a pretty girl I was. I would always get picked first when the teacher wanted to make an example of what a girl should be like. I would stand in front of our mirror and stare at my face, trying to figure out what they saw that was so beautiful about me. I soon developed a new appreciation for my uniquely dark skin out of the lenses of others who saw what I never saw. I realized then that there was only one Tade in the world, and I was the one. From that moment on I knew my life would be perfect.

4: My Life, My Story, My Determination

My perfect world came crashing down when my parents separated. I was only ten years old at the time and I remember very clearly returning home from boarding school one afternoon to meet my father packing up his belongings. I asked him where he was going this time, assuming he was off to one of his usual trips. He sat me down and told me he could not live with us any more. I asked why, staring at him in shock and disbelief. He replied, "Your mother does not want me here". I found that hard to believe because I knew how much my mother adored him in spite of his escapades.

After he moved out, I spent a lot of time crying because I wanted my father back home. I loved my father so much. He was my hero, my favorite person in the world. He treated me so specially and we had a very unique bond. My father was so cosmopolitan and modern. He had attended the University of Pittsburgh in Pennsylvania, and his thinking and ways of raising children were way different from the indigenous ways of our Yoruba tribe. He wanted his children to have a good western education, and he gave it to us. From the age of five my father who was an educationist introduced me to reading. He encouraged me to read and I remember anticipating his return from work everyday because I knew I would get a new book. I could not wait to finish one so I could get started on the next. Books made me come alive. I remember reading books written by different authors from all over the world and I would get lost in the books and imagine being there as the stories unfolded. After the separation of my parents, books became my escape. I read everything I could, I wrote poetry and short plays and watched as much television as my mother would allow. My favorite program to watch, besides the children's program, was the news. I loved to watch the women dress up in their beautiful African attire – they always looked so beautiful and so sophisticated. I wanted to be like them. At that time, it was my dream to become a television newscaster, but my father said no because they were supposedly 'loose women'.

It was also my dream to get my parents back together. My father would visit us (my two younger sisters and I) occasionally. I remember when he visited there was always so much tension. He would refuse to come into the house, so we would have to visit with him in his car. It made me sad that he would not speak to my mother, but I was always so overjoyed to see him that nothing else really mattered in that moment. I would beg him to come back home because I missed him so much. He said he could not come back home but we could come and stay with him but my mother would not allow it. My mother was a working woman. She was very strong and resilient. She worked for the Supreme Court of Nigeria at the time. After my father moved out, my grandmother moved in to help raise us. My father wanted her to give up custody of us to him because he felt he could give us a better life, but my mother refused. His partner at the time used to be a close friend of our family. She was a godmother to me and my younger brother who died at the age two and she was the reason my father left us. She had children of her own from a defunct marriage and my mother could not imagine this best friend-turned-traitor raising us with a sincere spirit.

Between the ages of ten and fifteen my sole purpose in life was to get my parents back together. The burden of their being reunited was put on me at such a tender age and I felt like a failure when I realized that my parents were not getting back together. As I grew up, I became angry and resentful about the situation. I desperately wanted my family back to the way it was--the Saturday family outings to the beach, the Sunday family lunch after church, the frequent visits to my grandmother together as a family, being dressed up in the morning and tucked into bed at night by my dad.

My sisters and I were always victims of the power struggle between my parents. They could never agree on any decisions that concerned us.

I remember when I was about to start high school. I was eager to start high school with my friends. My mother had picked that high school as the most popular and prestigious school in Lagos at the time, "Holy Child College". All of my friends were going to attend that same school, and I was very excited and happy. I especially looked forward to wearing the trendy school uniform. But, my father refused. He told my mother that I would be going to a federal government boarding school for girls outside Lagos, where I could get a better education, and become an important lady. He did not want me to become a newscaster/anchor, because in his opinion they had terrible reputations. When I arrived at that federal boarding school I was very homesick and angry, and for the first year I behaved badly academically and socially. I was angry because I was not with my friends. I was angry at my father's partner and her children for stealing my father away from us. I was consumed with anger and I felt helpless, so I spent most of my time reading and dreaming of traveling far away.

I finished high school and it was time for college. My

father wanted me close to home so I attended Lagos State University because it was located equidistant from both my parents homes. It was in college that I was finally relieved of the burden that I had carried for so many years. I was seventeen at this time and my uncle (who had lived in the United States since I was two years old) came home to visit. I shared my burden with him and he was the one who told me that my parents separation was not my fault and that bringing them back together was not my responsibility. As adults, we often do not always understand the impact of our words of encouragement and how it can affect or shape a child's life. My uncle (probably till the day he died) had no idea what his words did to me. I felt like a heavy weight had been lifted off my shoulders. I was free. I finished college a few years later. My dad and his mate had a bitter separation, I continued to miss the childhood I would have had if my parents had stayed together. Somehow I managed to get over the hurt and anger. I even released myself of the burden of unforgiveness that I had toward my father's mistress and her children (not my siblings).

As adults, we often do not always understand the impact of our words of encouragement and how it can affect or shape a child's life.

I carried the resentment for years because I felt they stole my father from my family, but now, even though my parents never got back together, I was finally at peace with the whole situation.

This experience inadvertently equipped me for the challenges I encountered later in life. There was the determination to survive and triumph despite the pain, conflict and anger.

5: Coming to America; My Life, My Dream

Getting married and having children was nowhere in my plans for the future. I was consumed with my family's situation for so long that I never gave it a thought, so what has happened to me is still so much a shocking experience. Life in Nigeria was easy for me. I did not have a care in the world. After college, I immediately started working at the bank. I lived at home with my mother and my two sisters. This was the normal practice at that time; young women like me did not move from their parents' home until they moved to their husbands' home. I still nursed my dream of being a news anchor, but the banking industry was exciting and financially rewarding.

It was a maddening rush to the top of your career and in a fast paced city like Lagos, hustling was the name of the game. I had bigger dreams; I wanted to see the world from a very early age. I had read books from different continents and this made me yearn to see the world that I read about in my books. I fell in love with a man who had the same dreams and for the first time in my life I imagined myself as somebody's wife. Marriage and motherhood had never crossed my mind until I met the man that God had ordained for me.

I graduated from the Lagos State University and began my mandatory one-year of government service with the National Youth Service Corp (NYSC). I was assigned to the United Bank of Africa. It was while I was in the NYSC that I met my husband. He was assigned to a medical clinic for his one year of mandatory service. We finished our year of government service in 1990 and got engaged two years later. Our dream was to rise to the top of our careers but not in Nigeria. We wanted a more relaxed life than the super cold calculated pace of Lagos, Nigeria, so we moved to the United States of America in 1992.

The corruption in Lagos was staggering, and people saw everything in terms of money. There was hardly any peace in Lagos. We had frequently heard that doctors could have a better chance of making a better life and career in the United States. In America, we had heard that there was peace, happiness, and joy. People could enjoy life without the constant hassle of business and schemes –that was what we were told.

When we arrived in New York City, we were shocked at

how similar it was to Lagos. We saw business and schemes everywhere in New York. People were not at peace. There was no joy and there was very little happiness. Overcrowding and people rushing everywhere was the order of the day. We could not tolerate that. So in six months, we moved to Chicago, Illinois. We arrived on the North side of Chicago but it was too crowded, so we quickly moved to the elite community of Hyde Park on Chicago's South-side near the University of Chicago. I got a job at the popular Citibank as a financial service officer. We did not want children right away, because we wanted to devote most of our time to our careers. We wanted the American way of life. We wanted to be laid back and enjoy peace.

We started working on having children a few years after we settled into our Hyde Park home. We tried for two years to no avail. Our families were beginning to wonder. The stares of my mother-in-law were burning, and my husband was so concerned about my not getting pregnant. We decided on a fertility expert, an African-American male who was wonderful. I got pregnant shortly thereafter. Having my first son made me appreciate and understand the nature of the love that my parents had for me. It was a profound feeling of love in a different dimension.

Five months after my first son was born, I got pregnant again. My second son not only changed my world, but he also changed how I view the world today. My relationship with my God has been taken to a much higher level and I view people a lot differently now, because of him. I am more tolerant and sympathetic towards others. I am no longer quick to judge the shortcomings of other people, instead, I am able to come up with excuses that help me to accept people for who they are. Since my son was born, I have gained tremendous insight into the intricacies and complexities of human behavior. I am no longer suspicious of people who behave differently from the norm. Instead, I have developed an affinity and an understanding for these groups of people. Now I teach my other children that God made all people differently and the difference does not only have to be in color, language or religion but also in behavior, responding to the environment, learning and daily interactions.

In all of my experiences, I have realized that you cannot trust people to see what you see, hear what you hear, feel what you feel or understand what you understand. You surely cannot expect them to do what you as a parent must do for your child. I learned very quickly that all my help came from God and Him alone. As I struggled to understand the callousness and unfeeling

> *You cannot trust people to see what you see; you cannot expect them to do what you as a parent must do for your child.*

attitude of the people around me, God told me that He will not share the glory of the healing of my child with anyone. From that moment, I stopped looking to people for help but I fixed my gaze upon Jesus – the author and the finisher of my son's life. God has worked His many miracles through numerous people and I must acknowledge that he has sent us all wonderful therapists, who themselves have been amazed at the kind of progress that my son has made. They all see something unique in my son and are mostly amazed at his intelligence and potential. This is a child, so fearfully and wonderfully made by God, that even experts cannot fail to recognize God at work in his development.

I have learned that children are a reward from God, but you have to be careful and understand that everyone does not feel this way. Some people feel that if your child is different from most then they are a curse, and not a reward. If you do not understand this, then you are in store for a lot of unnecessary hurt and frustration, especially as you try to parent a child with unique needs.

Children are a reward from God, but not everyone feels this way.

Every day of my life is a learning field. I learn the good, the bad and the ugly. Above all, I learn that all things work together for the good of those who love the Lord. I have learnt to take every new experience in stride. I learn from every situation that comes my way. Each new day comes with different challenges, and in the institution of life, we come across and overcome new challenges every day. You never know what the day is going to bring. It is like unwrapping a present everyday. That is why I put my trust in God and call on Him every morning to guide me in the right path. I ask Him to help me make the right decisions in every situation. In this world of autism, the parent is vulnerable not knowing who to trust, desperate for a cure, eager to try the next new thing that promises to bring some relief to the daily pain and struggle that they face.

6: A Prince is Born

My second pregnancy was a joyous time of anticipation for my husband and I. Our first child was now a beautiful, healthy, normal five-month-old boy, and we could hardly wait to experience the joy of another child just like him.

Our second child was born exactly thirteen months after our first. We were overjoyed with the idea of having two babies after waiting and trying for what seemed like eternity. Shortly after I discovered I was having another child, I took a leave of absence from my job at the bank. The timing of the pregnancy came at the same time that I was terribly disappointed with a situation at my job. A wonderful new position (Loan Officer) became available, and a young African American female and I were the top two candidates for the position. She got the position, and I believe to this day that she got the position because I was an immigrant from Nigeria. I was constantly tired from the demands of my job and it became increasingly difficult to cope with work. I had a five month old and another baby on the way. The leave of absence was a perfect idea. The bank approved the leave and I went home to work on my growing family.

I had an uneventful pregnancy for the most part. There was however one incident that I will never forget and till this day it still comes to my thoughts. Could it have been a clue that we missed? About six months into my pregnancy, I had an ultrasound at the Illinois Masonic Hospital. Throughout the ultrasound, which lasted over an hour, I noticed that my baby was very calm and peaceful; he just laid still not moving and he had his thumb in his mouth. This totally amazed me because I remember my first son was so active during his ultrasound, he would not keep still for a minute. The ultrasound for my third child was similar to that of my first. When I think back to that event, I cannot help but wonder if that was a sign. I remember being in the room for a long period of time, while the technicians and the doctors consulted and discussed. There was never any mention to me about anything being wrong with the baby and at the time it did not seem like I should have been worried.

During the last few weeks of my pregnancy, I tested positive for the Streptococcus A infection and I was told that I would be given antibiotics during the delivery. This would ensure that I did not pass on the infection to the baby. The day after my son was born, my OB/GYN and the Pediatrician that was assigned to my baby tried to convince my husband and I about giving the baby a blood transfusion since they believed the baby might have gotten the infection.

We declined the transfusion based on my husband's judgment as a physician. Again, I felt there was nothing to worry about. I do not doubt the competence of all those who were involved with my pregnancy and my son's delivery. However, when you find yourself in certain situations, you cannot help but think back on every single detail to see if you missed something. You frequently ask yourself what you have done wrong. *Why me? What could have gone wrong to cause this? Why me? Why my son? No, not my son!*

When our first son Ayodeji Michael Oluwatobiloba was born, we thought we could never love another child as much as we loved him. Then came Ayoyinka Immanuel, not quite as feisty as Ayodeji, but he made his entrance with such calm and presence that you could not help but notice that royalty had been born. Ayoyinka Immanuel Odunayo came into this world with a regal style weighing 8 pounds and 12 ounces, 11:55am Christmas morning 1997.

We were completely overwhelmed with joy. I was unquestionably an African Queen mother. I had given birth to two whole and beautiful sons. The sky had again returned close to the earth and the people were all very happy. But Ayoyinka was such a quiet baby, and so less active than his

45

older brother. We were so excited about watching our two boys growing up together and playing together. I was so sure that they would grow up to be the best of friends, and they could 'watch out' and care for each other in this land far from the place where we were born. We just assumed Ayoyinka's quietness was a part of his personality, so we were not concerned about his development. He often looked so serious and he rarely smiled.

When Yinka turned six months, I went back to work at the bank, but it was not the same. My return to work only lasted six months. I wanted more challenge. Yinka was such an easy infant to care for. The day before Yinka's first birthday, I quit my job at the bank and enrolled in a full-time evening MBA program at the Governor's State University. It seemed to me that it was the best decision I could have made. I spent time with the boys and studied during the day, and went to school in the evening. The pace of my life was really stepped up and I felt like God was working a special plan in my life. I just did not know what the plan was. It was about six months into my MBA program, at the same time Yinka turned eighteen months of age, that it seemed like the bottom suddenly fell out of the plan God had for my life. Although I still did not know what plan God had for me.

I was totally blindsided by the whirlwind that consumed me and completely disrupted the homeostasis that existed within my family.

7: Beginning of School Runs

We felt that Yinka was growing and developing normally until his scheduled eighteen-month check-up visit with his pediatrician, Dr. Ansuah Shah, at Rush Hospital. Dr. Shah was the pediatrician for both of our sons. She asked, "How many words does he say?" I was shocked at my answer. Two words! Was that all? It was then that I realized that he had never said the words, Mama or Dada. In church, he always echoed the words Hallelujah and Glory but it never occurred to me that he had not developed any spontaneous words. She gave us a referral to an early childhood educational resource within the hospital.

Her referral opened up a whole new world of pediatric therapies (speech therapy, physical therapy, occupational therapy, play therapy, nutritional therapy, music therapy etc). The bottom fell out of my plan for taking care of my family and going to evening school, because now I had to take Yinka for early childhood educational classes in the afternoon. At the time, I did not realize that I had suddenly embarked on a slow and painful journey of learning about my child the hard way.

The way I understood it, Yinka would start communicating normally after a few early intervention classes. There was no cause for alarm. It was after that visit in Dr. Shah's office that I started asking family and friends about how long it takes before children start talking. How many words should they have? Everyone I talked to just brushed it off, and some told me stories of children who never spoke until they were about five years of age.

By the time he was two years of age, I began to become worried about his development. The worry persisted for three years and he was five years old, when finally, we sat motionless in the office of my son's pediatrician as he announced that our son had autism. For a long while, I was emotionally paralyzed. I began a frantic search for the meaning of "autism". My son was beginning to behave in some unusual ways, which put a real strain on the family's normal way of doing things. I was beginning to frequently question God. What had I done to deserve this? Why did my child have to be born so different?

I kept hoping that Yinka would grow out of this "silence". I started praying that he would grow out of this silence, because I knew that he would. The pediatrician had made us aware of what we already knew but now we were concerned that it might be a real problem, a "speech delay" that we had no idea of what to do about it.

The people in our community began to frown when we came around. Shame was haunting me, and fear had me so confused. We decided to try putting him in preschool, so he could get special educational help. For a while in the beginning, it appeared to be working well until I became aware of the racism and general confusion about autism in the educational community. The thought of my son being like this for the rest of his life nearly scared me to death. What would happen to him when he grew up? How would he take care of himself? Who would take care of him if something happened to us, his parents? I needed help, urgently! I prayed for help. My son was now five years old, and his school placement was becoming unbearable. I began to hate to see him go to school.

The whole concept of a speech delay in a young child was totally foreign to me. In my mind, you have a baby and they grow and do what every baby does. Babies are expected to crawl at a certain age. Babies are expected to sit alone at a certain age. Babies are expected to walk at a certain age. And of course babies are expected to talk at a certain age. My Yinka was no different from other babies. The pediatrician had advised us to enroll Yinka in an Early Intervention (EI) program for infants, toddlers, and young children who were handicapped or at risk for a handicap. We took the pediatrician's advice and enrolled Yinka in an EI in our school district.

My hopes and anticipation that Yinka would be all right soon gave way to the reality that my Yinka was indeed different from his older brother. It was like an unknown fear came to our doorstep and was knocking hard on our door. I went to the door but I would not open it. *Who are you? What do you want?* I asked these questions over and over.

I began to see Yinka much differently. At home and at birthday parties he would go off and play by himself. He always avoided a crowd. I would wonder why he was sitting all by himself, away from everyone. I tried hard to teach Yinka to talk. I bought books, videos and computer learning softwares and I would work with Yinka for hours everyday. The teachers at the EI program were frequently talking about something called "autism". I did not know what they were talking about. One day a teacher even told me a story about an autistic person named Temple Grandin, but that name was unfamiliar to me and I did not pay much attention to it. I continued to worry about Yinka's development. My son was getting older and growing stronger in his unusual ways. Our social life was being challenged, and my spirit was being tried.

We enrolled Yinka in the Calvary Day Care at two years of age, but they "kicked him out" within a month because he would not sit in the group. So I took him to "Stepping Stones," another preschool program, but they "kicked him out" in two weeks because he would not take a nap. Then I took him to Kiddies Kollege, another preschool program, where he stayed for six months. He still would not take a nap, and the teacher called and said that I would have to come and stay with him while he took a nap. They also started to complain about him not being potty trained and he was about 30 months. We were making a brief trip to Nigeria but I knew this would be the end for Yinka at Kiddies Kollege, so when we got back from the trip to Nigeria, I started looking for another place for Yinka.

I found a place called "Big Bear", a center owned by HOPE, an organization that also owned an adult developmental center. They were a big help in being able to handle him, and he stayed there until he was three years of age. Yinka's speech delay had not changed, but he was three now and he could go to regular public school. I knew the public school could help Yinka.

When Yinka turned three he was now old enough to be enrolled in the public school near our home in South Holland, Illinois. It was the MacArthur School, and he was placed in the half-day special education preschool program, from 9 to 12 noon. In the afternoon I would take him back to the "Big Bear". I trusted the school. I knew they could help my Yinka because they were the official school. They had all the educational professionals. I still wanted Yinka to have a regular school experience. He was in class with children that behaved like him or worse than him. The class had children with different types of diagnosis ranging from autism to down syndrome and cerebral palsy. Every child came with different needs and different, sometimes severe, behaviors. It was difficult for Yinka to model any positive behavior instead he modeled the negative behaviors like tantrums and screaming. This disturbed me greatly so I decided to enroll him in the Montessori school that my older son attended. The school was very supportive and my son's teacher took him into her class for a few hours a day. This went on for a whole semester. Looking back, I wish I had let him stay on but he was finally going into the full day program at MacArthur and the Montessori teacher wanted us to wait till October before he could start back the new school year. The arrangement was not feasible since Yinka liked consistency and breaking his routine midway would have caused a major setback for him. That ended the Montessori era.

I enrolled for an evening MBA program at the Governors State University. I did not know what to expect from Yinka's school, but I looked for change in him everyday.

When I did not see real change in him after a year, I asked for more time in getting help from the special educators and related services. I wanted to see him learning how to be normal. I wanted him to learn life skills, but Yinka was not trying to learn them. He was not trying to learn how to bath himself. The school told me that he was getting the most time that he could get, so I started trying to teach him myself. We went back to the pediatrician's office because we were getting anxious. The school was not giving him enough speech therapy and we felt he needed more services than he was getting. We asked the pediatrician if she could give us a referral for speech therapy and she did. We were given an appointment for three months from the time of our referral. This is another challenge that most parents face. They have to wait 3-6 months for an appointment. They have to wait for all those months to get answers to their questions. In most cases, there is a waiting list for appointments and then for services. We waited 3 months and then came the day of the appointment.

Ours was at the Rush University Teaching Hospital. There I was, a naïve parent in a room full of students, unknown to me. They tried to get Yinka to do a lot of things, but he would not even sit in the chair long enough to cooperate. After about an hour of struggle, the students finally told me that they would want me to make another appointment to see the speech pathologist in three months. They said she could not see me that day because she had a class to teach. I was quite upset at the thought of waiting another three months. I demanded to speak with her. I was shocked when she came into the room and told me that based on the report of her students she did not think there was any amount of speech therapy that would help my son.

I walked out of that hospital that day determined never to return and determined to prove her wrong. Parents wait and live for those appointments like that will be the solution to their problems. To have waited all those months and to hear such negativity and discouragement is the most crushing experience for any parent. From that moment I decided not to allow my son to get lost in any bureaucratic system. I decided to find help where I could. There had to be more out there than hospitals had to offer. There was a lot of research going on and our children were being used as guinea pigs. I truly appreciate the work of doctors and hospitals but some of us parents are racing against time and every minute wasted can be detrimental to the future of our child(ren). While most moms like me were busy being soccer Moms and driving their kids to different activities. I became a therapy mom and drove my son to any therapeutic program that we felt would help him

8: Diagnosis or Misdiagnosis

The teachers at MacArthur School were quite helpful. The school nurse had mentioned to me about a grant that was available, that enabled the school to bring in a pediatric neuropsychiatrist to the school to evaluate some of the children. Yinka was one of the children to be seen by Dr. Berry Kravis.

It was during that visit after a series of questions, tests and observations that the pediatrician announced, "Your son has PDD (Pervasive Developmental Disorder). She explained it to mean speech delay, developmental delay and symptoms of autism. For a long while I was emotionally paralyzed, there goes that strange word being thrown out again. Even though I did not know what the word meant, the look on the pediatrician's face was all I needed to know it was a terrible condition. One day I could not take the worry and not knowing any longer, so I walked into the South Holland Library and asked if they had any books on autism. There must have been fifty books, so I borrowed about ten of them because that was all I could carry at the time. Boy! Did I ask for trouble? It was as though I had opened "Pandora's Box". When I opened the first book I could not put it down until I had finished reading it. The shock and horror of my son's condition hit me that day. I could not believe that I had been sitting in such an explosive condition. That day was the beginning of an emotional roller coaster ride for me.

Each book described conditions that by now were so familiar to me. No eye contact, not wanting to be touched, disliked gentle strokes only deep pressures or tight grips, preferred to be alone and seemed to enjoy solitude, crying, screaming and throwing tantrums for no apparent reason, tiptoeing around the house, lining everything up in order, very independent and tried to do everything himself because he did not know how to ask, restlessness, constantly on the move. Finally, I felt I was not alone (some other people out there understood what I was going through). Each book I opened revealed a whole new idea, a different concept and various treatments available to me.

Now I was on a mission to try everything that was available. I was determined to make my son better. I was determined to give my first son what other children had, a normal relationship with their sibling.

Even as a toddler, I knew my oldest son missed being able to play normally with his younger brother.

When Yinka turned four he was enrolled in the full day program where he was being bused from home to school everyday. This is when we were first introduced to the concept of an IEP (Individual Education Plan). The whole team of educators including my husband and I got together to discuss and draw up goals for Yinka's education. I must say that a great number of the terminologies used at the IEP meeting were foreign to me. For the most part we just sat there and listened. When we were asked what goals we had for our son, the only goal we had was that he would speak. For parents out there, you have as much say in the education of your special child as the educators do. I urge you not to be intimidated by their wealth of knowledge. They are professionals, but never hesitate to stop them and ask questions when you do not understand. Make notes at the meetings then go home and carry out your research. Liaise with other parents, read all the literature that you can lay your hands on. You are the best advocate your child will ever have. The most well meaning educator is bound by educational and district laws that may not allow them to serve your child to the best of their ability. Funding for special education is very limited in some states like Illinois and certain school districts. If you have a child with special needs, it is important that you research the schools in the neighborhood where you live or wish to buy a home. Parents of children with special needs have practically sold their homes, given up their jobs and moved to a different state in search of a school district that better served children with unique challenges. Bear in mind that as much as that teacher loves your child and wants to help, they will not risk losing their job fighting for services on behalf of your child. They can be easily intimidated by the school system, but you cannot. As a parent, you have rights and so does your child. Oftentimes, the goal that educators have for your child is different from your expectations. The average parent is looking for a cure, not so much a quick fix, but a situation where your child is able to live a normal and independent life and survive in a society that will not give them a chance if they are not deemed normal.

The educators however are trained to keep these children engaged until they are 22, at which age the state is no longer responsible for their education. They want to give the children a free and appropriate public education, but in most cases as a parent, you have to fight for the appropriateness of the education that your child will receive.

Another challenge that I faced (and I am sure a lot of parents are facing with the schools) was that the educators had very low expectations of my son and they seemed to teach him according to what they felt was his ability.

I have worked with my son since I discovered that he had a challenge and I resolved to teach him as much as I could and introduce him to as many concepts as I could. Having worked with my son, I knew his capabilities. So you can imagine how frustrating it is when a teacher tells you at an IEP meeting that he is not able to do certain things that you know he is able to do or is already doing. I appreciate the effort of special education teachers, and I must say that some of them are very creative. However, others really try to put your child in a box and hand them the kind of education they deem best for them. They try to convince you that your child is not ready for certain topics and the real reason is that they are reluctant to put the extra effort to find out if the child can do it or not. Our children spend a good part of their day in school and it is a shame that they do not get the maximum benefit that they should from the school. Parents that have a choice get their children extra help from outside the school. All I wanted was to hear the sound of my son's voice. For years, I did not know what Yinka's voice sounded like and I found myself often imagining how it would sound the first time he called me mommy.

School was very challenging for Yinka. The teacher constantly reported his inability to sit in his chair and his refusal to participate in circle time. At some point, they had to put him in a chair with restraints just to make him sit still. My frustrations grew as I realized that he was not sitting still enough to learn anything. There was certainly not enough time in the day for the teacher or the assistant to sit with Yinka. This would have been at the expense of the nine other children in the classroom. On my several observations of the classroom, I realized that my son was being ignored and he was not allowed to participate in activities due to his behavior. This upset me and I voiced my concern to the classroom teacher. Finally, the teacher requested for an aide for Ayoyinka. The presence of a one-on-one aide enabled him access to the curriculum to some extent. There was also the issue of the noises he was making constantly. By the age of four, he would constantly throw himself to the ground and throw a tantrum for no apparent reason or when he was not allowed to have his way. This seemed to distract the children and disrupt classroom activities. These behaviors were also occurring at home and at the store. At home, he became obsessed with TV commercials and practically threw a tantrum after every commercial. We later discovered that the noise from the TV, the movement in the store and the activity of the classroom played a major role in triggering the tantrums.

We started to turn down the volume of the TV at home or turn it completely off. I avoided going shopping with the boys and had to wait till my husband got home late at night to do my grocery shopping. Thank God, the store by my house closed at midnight. At school, the therapist suggested that Yinka should wear headphones and listen to some classical music. He also wore a weighted vest while in the classroom and this seemed to help him calm down. His preschool teacher at the time, had a lot of knowledge about children with autism and she tried different things with Yinka.

One thing that struck me and also made me uncomfortable was the fact that Yinka remained in the same classroom for three years straight. I was concerned that the progress he was making was tremendously slow. At age five, there were certain milestones I expected him to have reached and he still had not. I became restless and started to look at other schools – private, public and therapeutic day schools.

9: The Due Process

It was a constant battle with the schools. At McArthur school, Yinka was in class with children of various ages and different disabilities. As he got older, the classroom grew less challenging for him. He began to get restless again and stopped paying attention. We finally settled for a more self-contained class at another school called ECHO. The curriculum was more advanced. It looked like a real classroom setting and Yinka was in a class with his age appropriate peers.

At Echo, there seemed to be more structure and things worked out for a while until Yinka's behavior started to earn him time outside of the class. The teacher complained constantly and she would have him sit outside the class several times a day. At this report, I felt that he was not learning anything by sitting out in the hallway for the most part of the day. The new teacher was quite intolerant and she did not make any effort to get to know Yinka. She sent several notes home that confirmed her irritation. She would not allow him to go on field trips with the group and my husband and I sensed that our son was being ostracized from the class. His classroom aide was not being utilized and so he was not able to access the curriculum. We were told that Yinka was being removed from the class because his behaviors were disruptive. He made loud noises and would not pay attention in a group or complete his work.

The school psychologist requested a meeting with us and inquired about placing Yinka on medication. The fact was that Yinka had been on medication prior to starting this new school . We had started him on the stimulant Ritalin to improve his focus, attention and reduce the hyperactivity and impulsivity. The medication had adverse effects on Yinka. It made him walk around like a zombie. When he started to hallucinate, we took him off the medication. There was however an upside to the medication. Yinka lost his appetite and lost a lot of weight which was a good thing considering his abnormal body mass index.

The school had been notified of his use of medication, and when we told them he was no longer using it, they attributed his behavior to the lack of medication. The teacher became even more intolerant because we refused to drug our son and make her job easier. This drew the battle line and the beginning of the long road to the due process hearing. We had no control over the classroom and the way our son was treated. The fact of the matter was that his classroom aide was being utilized by the teacher to assist other students and this took away from the personal attention Yinka needed. If she stayed with him as was specified in his IEP, his behavior would be less disruptive. All he needed was redirection to help him stay focused and on task. On several occasions when I visited the classroom, the aide was not present. The mood in the class was always hostile and tense. At that point, I knew I had to do something drastic. I requested for a due process hearing based on the fact that Yinka was being refused a free and appropriate public education. He was denied access to the class and his aide was utilized for tasks that did not include working with him.

Since Yinka was spending most of his time in school outside the classroom. We decided to keep him at home and try homeschooling. We put Yinka on a schedule and he seemed to be doing well at home. We got some push-back from the school district as they notified us that we could not keep him out of school. This caused us to initiate a due process.

Due process is a formal way to resolve disputes with a school about your child's education. You can file a due process complaint only for special education disputes, not for

In the U.S., you can file a due process complaint for special education disputes.

general education issues. You have the right to an impartial hearing officer and to present evidence and witnesses at the due process hearing.

A parent can request for a due process hearing when they feel that their children are not getting the service that they need especially if those services were specified in the Individual Education Plan (IEP). Most parents do not even realize that their children have this right.

There is a lot of intimidation that goes on within school districts. Parents are treated like they do not have a say in their child's education because they are not professionals. As a parent, you are the only real and effective advocate that your child has. No one can fight for your child like you can. Teachers love parents that stay away from their classrooms and do not meddle in the education of their children.

I realized that if he was home-schooled, the school would lose the funding that was allocated for my child's education. I became so frustrated that I wanted to sue the school for not making my son the way that I wanted him to be. We went through with the due process hearing and a mediator was assigned to oversee the case. The school admitted that they had made a mistake, and begged for an opportunity to correct their wrong. We were not happy with the outcome of the meeting and we realized that nothing was going to change. My husband and I went home and made a decision to sell our house and move to a district that would be more favorable to our child's education. We bought a home in the North suburbs and quickly realized that the same problem existed in this new district.

As we struggled to settle into the new school district, we realized that Yinka's new "Individualized Educational Program" (IEP) could not follow him to the new school. He would have to have a new program, and the old fears that had been born at the old school began to creep into my head. Would the new school be like the old school? Would they deprive my son of a "free and appropriate education"? I said to myself, "Now that I know what my son needs in terms of interventions to be more normal, I must make sure he gets them."

The first day at the new school was a 'day-out-of-hell'. There had been a mistake from the old school. His IEP had not been updated because of his constant struggles. The school report graded his level of functioning much lower than his ability. The new district therefore placed him in a class with lower functioning children that could not stimulate growth in Yinka. Within a few weeks we saw him regress in his behavior and adaptive functions. It was another mad rush to get him placed in the right learning environment. We knew we had rights that the school must obey. So, I wrote a letter asking that our rights not be violated and my son be given a "free and appropriate education" in this new school district. After the school read the letter they apologized for making a mistake and again my son was on the road to getting the intervention services he needed. Bureaucratic frustrations set in again as we were informed that he would have to stay in the current classroom for forty-five days. They needed to perform a new assessment on him, which was a good thing. The new teachers believed that he was in a wrong learning environment and a new assessment would give them a clearer baseline of his cognitive functioning and abilities. We settled into the new learning environment and things went well until we realized that Yinka was not given speech therapy for months. It was stated clearly on his IEP, but there were issues with the therapist taking some time off and there was no replacement provided for her absence. The children were therefore denied a free and appropriate public education due to an administrative glitch. I did not have the tolerance for bureaucratic flaws where my son's future was concerned. He was only getting one hour of speech therapy every week, so realizing that he was deprived of that was devastating. The school needed to make this up another way. We once again went to due process with the school and the results were unfavorable. We realized that we had to take matters into our own hands. God had blessed us with resources and we decided (like most parents who could afford services outside the school) to seek extra services that would enrich our son's life. We decided to enroll him in private speech therapy, occupational therapy, music therapy, swimming lessons, music lessons and any other extracurricular activities that his brothers were involved in.

In the midst of the struggle with the school district in South Holland, I became pregnant with my third child. Ayokitan Christopher Ayobamiji was born 4 years and 3 months after his brother.

By the time we moved to the north suburbs, I had three boys under the age of 10. My youngest son was about 3 years old. Yinka was 7 and Deji was 8. Raising 3 boys while dealing with one that had special needs was quite challenging. Trying to balance the special programs for Yinka while ensuring that his two brothers did not lack anything in terms of love, attention and social participation was a huge undertaking. I was the Soccer/Therapy mom. I had to drag my kids everywhere. I hoped they would not resent their brother for taking up so much time and energy.

It was a real struggle and my life metamorphosed into something I could never have imagined. I was stressed, irritable, short-tempered and just frustrated. I felt unsupported, unappreciated and undervalued. My whole life was consumed with this Enigma called Autism. No one around me knew what I was going through. I was a ball of emotions. My other two boys literally conformed to my wishes and would comply with any demands. There was no room for arguments. If it was time to go to therapy. Everyone knew to get dressed and get in the car with no questions asked and no argument. It was not a question of whether they wanted to go, they had no choice. We would do homework in the therapist's office while we waited for Yinka to finish his session. My boys knew that I expected them to be of good behavior. In hindsight, I believe part of their childhood was taken from them. People would not invite them to parties because they did not want their brother to come along. My oldest son would not invite friends over from school because he felt embarrassed by his brother. It was a tough time for a pre-adolescent who was growing through stages of Erikson's psychosocial stages of development. At this stage of industry vs inferiority, children between ages 6-12 years compare themselves to peers to see how they measure up. According to Erikson, children move into the identity vs confusion stage at about age 12, where they are faced with questions of identity, developing a sense of self and certain complexities of life, like having a sibling with autism. When he turned eleven, we sent him to a prestigious boarding school in Nigeria for three years. We felt this would give him a sense of identity that was separated from the burden he felt from conforming to our needs whether he agreed or not. I worried about how his brother's autism affected him. How lonely he must feel not having a friend/confidant in his brother. He found solace in a group of friends from the church that he grew up with and still holds those relationships dear to this day. The relationships he could not have with his brother, he was able to develop with this group of young men.

10: I Will Try Anything

The first book I read was about changing the diet, I started with the Gluten and Casein free diet. And I tried every recipe in the book. I discovered a health food store close to my house and I became the most frequent customer. I was in there everyday asking questions, buying every Gluten and Casein free food, snack and drink. I totally changed my son's diet. He ate it for a while but after a few weeks he stopped eating the food. I figured he got tired of it and frankly it tasted awful.

Next, we discovered a clinic out in Naperville, Illinois. The Pfeiffer institute used vitamins to treat autism so we went and paid thousands of dollars to get bottles of enzymes, yeast, cod liver oil, and we would practically force them down Yinka's throat. We would hide it in applesauce, yogurt and juice but he would always taste the vitamins. It was a frustrating experience.

Our next stop was the Son-Rise Program, taught at the Option Institute's Autism Treatment Center of America in Western Massachusetts. Having a child with Autism can be isolating, but as you take a seat on the floor of the lecture hall with hundreds of parents, you immediately feel a sense of kinship. The program focused on using the holistic approach to help draw out children with low functioning autism. Halfway through the course, we realized that our boy Yinka was past that stage. Since we had invested thousands of dollars again, we completed the program and returned home ambivalent but hopeful. We tried to implement the program but we were unable to sustain the demands of the program and it did not seem right for a child whose functioning was beyond the severe cases targeted at the program.

We applied for the Advocate Puente's program and we were placed on the waiting list for almost a year. I was not going to put my child's life on hold for a year, waiting for a spot that may never open up. We decided to explore other programs and we found the Sertoma speech and hearing center. At the Sertoma center, Yinka would not sit in the chair long enough to receive any productive service. I was frustrated and the therapists were at a loss of what to do. I watched as they helplessly struggled to get him to sit and attend. What happened to innovation and taking time to figure out what works best for this particular child?

When Yinka turned 5, we went to the Advocate center for pediatric development where we finally got a proper diagnosis of autism. Then we were still on the waiting list for the Puentes program. While we waited, they were able to fit us into a less intensive program called the Camino's program. This program started with a parent training program that was mandatory before your child could be enrolled in the actual program. After the training, we enrolled Yinka in the occupational and behavior therapy program at the Advocate clinic. This went on for months, but we still could not get speech therapy which was the focus of the Puentes program. For us, speech was the driving force because our goal of therapy was for Yinka to learn to talk and no one was offering us that solution.

We found another program Pediatric potentials where things seemed to go well for a while until he started getting restless. The problem with this place was that it was a training ground for speech therapy and occupational therapy students. There was a high turnover in the staff and for a child with autism, the lack of consistency could be very overwhelming. Soon Yinka got restless and stopped paying attention. It seemed that as soon as he was finally getting used to a therapist, adjusting and making progress, there would be a new person and we would have to start over.

Eventually, I realized that I was driving one hour twice a week to the North side of Chicago from my south suburban home for no real results.

While Yinka attended Pediatric Potentials, I discovered a parent training program that was run in the same building called Tuesdays Child. You were assigned a mentor who is also a parent and had completed the program. I learnt a lot from these parents about schools and how to handle behaviors. It was like a behavior modification program. At that time, we were already having serious behavior problems with Yinka. The tantrums were endless and it was at this place that I learnt about adjusting the environment of the child to help him cope better. It was such a relief when we realized that just turning down the noise from the TV or completely turning it off made a whole lot of difference in our home.

I began to realize that I was embarking on a long, frustrating and hard south journey. I had absolutely no help from anyone; no one understood what I was going through. People around who saw the struggle conveniently walked on by. I seemed to be running around from pillar to post looking for help for my son. I felt like it was a race against time. I had to get him fixed before he turned a certain age, where his behavior would be unmodifiable.

It was almost impossible to find a facility for speech and occupational therapy in the South suburbs; they either had a long waiting list or it was too far away. I poured myself more into my studies and research for a cure and the more I found myself in this struggle alone, the more I learnt to lean on God, to trust in Him and call on Him. The arm of flesh will fail you but the arms of God are everlasting arms. He said, "I will never leave you or forsake you." I was totally dependent on God because He was all I had.

Then, I heard about a Speech-Language Pathologist who was in a nearby city. I called him and made an appointment. On the day of the appointment, as I sat in the waiting room, a strange feeling of warm relief came over me. In the appointment interview he talked about new technologies that can retrain or rewire the human brain, so people can become more normal. There is hope for my son "to be made new again". A lot of educational changes must be made on my son's "Individualized Educational Program" if we are to be successful. This was when I met face-to-face with the complex laws and rules that apply to special education in this country. Brady Language Academy is where we finally found some ray of hope. After a few months, Yinka said his first full sentence, "I want to eat". Arnell Brady is an accomplished African-American, Speech and Language Pathologist. He was God-sent. For the first time, someone saw my son for what he could be and not what he was. Someone took the time to talk to me as a mother and encourage my husband and I through the difficult ordeal. Brady Speech and Language therapy became our routine every week for almost 10 years. At this center, we were introduced to a whole new method of therapy. It was a method that Yinka was all too familiar with - Computer-based therapy. Since he was eighteen months old, I had exposed Yinka to educational software like reader rabbit, knowledge adventure and the learning company. Therefore, when he was introduced to the Fast Forward family of products, he had no problems at all adapting. Brady language academy offered technological advance treatment. After a few years, living with autism became a way of life. Once we had all the plates spinning at once, we became more hopeful.

At the entrance of the 21st century came scientific breakthroughs in the cure for autism. Yinka had been on the Fast Forword program for 3 years and he made tremendous progress. This computer-based program addresses auditory processing and stimulation. He progressed through the levels from language acquisition to reading and over the years his speech emerged. In conjunction with the speech therapy, we tried other computer based programs like Captain log, Interactive Metronome. We also added physical and occupational therapy to Yinka's routine. We installed a Brachiation Ladder in our basement.

The benefits of brachiation include the development of manual skill, improvement of intelligence, extension of the rib cage, and greater thoracic extension means more oxygen for the brain. It aids in the improvement of breathing and oxygenation. It helps in the increase in the strength of the hands and arms. It also helps in the proper development of the back, better definition of the laterality of the brain, greater ease and dexterity when writing, improvement of visual convergence and optimal development of eye-hand coordination.

There are many benefits the Brachiation Ladder offers.

We also saw a child psychiatrist at La Rabida Hospital who recommended behavior management. The doctor also prescribed a stimulant to help reduce the symptoms of hyperactivity, impulsivity and inattention. The medication made Yinka calm but he lost his appetite, lost weight and began to have hallucinations.

After our ordeal with the school districts, we decided to try Applied Behavior Analysis (ABA). We found the North Shore Pediatric Center where we met Dr. John Smagner, who helped us set up a home program. Yinka received ABA for about 5 years and this helped him tremendously. Yinka has received ABA therapy since September 2006 and it is amazing what this has done for him. When I look at him

I can hardly remember those years when all I wanted was to hear the sound of his voice. Now, he is able to answer simple questions and we are working on conversational language. With autism, you can never give up hope of a normal life for your child. Hope is what keeps you going and wakes you up every morning.

As we found solace in therapy, we married it with extracurricular activities. As Yinka moved from elementary to middle school and then to high school, we began to appreciate the plethora of resources that existed in the town that we lived in. We were introduced to the Evanston Special Recreation during my search for summer programs that transcended summer school. The Evanston Special Recreation has been a life saver for us. Since he was about 12, Yinka has participated in swimming, basketball, volleyball, powerlifting, track and field, bowling and numerous sporting activities. He has taken part in the Special Olympics several times and has won several medals. We discovered that keeping him engaged with a predictable schedule has helped to keep him calm and grounded. He knows what to anticipate. His schedule is like clockwork and you have to explain to him in advance why his schedule is changing.

11: When Your Community Lets You Down

My family was very involved in our local church and this was a very important aspect of our lives. My husband and I were both raised by Christian mothers and doing God's work was instilled in us at a very early age. We intended to pass this on to our children . My son's autism threw me into a deep relationship with Christ. I believe that God can heal my child and he can be made whole just like the miracles that Jesus worked in the Bible. This kept me going and with each triumph and improvement, I gave glory to God. I was determined to not allow my situation hinder me from serving God.

Unfortunately, not everyone understood what it meant to have a child with a disability. My church was a community church with 90 percent of its membership being of Nigeria descent. The reality was that though we lived in the United States, what we gained in the western culture in terms of available resources we lacked in terms of support from our community. This was a church community where people felt a sense of belonging and kinship. But it was an extension of the world where I grew up. I turned to my church and they turned away, and I could not stop my tears from flowing. The average person in my church did not know the word Autism. In the world we grew up in, children like my son had no place in society. They were not taken into public places and were mostly kept away from curious stares. Having a child with a disability was a taboo in our culture. It was never discussed or acknowledged. I was faced with yet another battle of my life.

What do you do when your community lets you down? This, after all, is the United States. Everyone should be more exposed and more tolerant. I learned the hard way that people did not have the patience or the tolerance to put up with your issues. A child with a disability made people in my community look deep into themselves and most people preferred to portray their shallow and perfect persona, amidst the stares, the whispers, the judgments and outright confrontations. You pull yourself up by the bootstraps and keep on moving. I had the conviction to not leave the church even when I did not feel supported. I threw myself into God's work and decided to help my son integrate into this part of our lives. Having a child with unique

> *I learned the hard way that people did not have the patience or the tolerance to put up with your issues.*

needs can be a very lonely experience if the people in your community have a limited understanding of what you are going through.

One Wednesday service, an individual asked if people with mental disabilities were made in the image of God. And I listened in amazement as the pastors struggled to find the appropriate answer to the question. Attempts to integrate my son into church programs by hiring a private tutor that could work with him during church services was met with prejudice and bureaucracy. Some days it was so frustrating amidst all the pressures that I felt like giving up or getting away to a place far away.

I joined the prayer group in church as prayer was the only department that helped me maintain my sanity. The prayer group was my support group. We prayed together, fasted together and encouraged one another.

Since my son did not fit into any classroom and most of the teachers rejected him, I decided to start a special needs class in my church with another parent. There were 3 other children with autism in the church and the parents felt the same frustration as I did. This decision was met with push-back from the coordinators in the children's church. Some of them felt that my son was being given preferential treatment because my husband and I were ministers in the church and they did not understand why he should have a classroom all to himself. We pushed past that ignorance and created a classroom where the children could express themselves and learn about God. Due to my experience with feeling unsupported, I started a support group for parents of children with special needs. We pray every Thursday for

Due to my experience with feeling unsupported, I started a support group for parents of children with special needs.

our children and then we answer questions or share experiences that help parents who are struggling with their children's disabilities. When you have a child with special needs, prayers are endless. You never lose hope, you never lose faith, you keep trusting and hoping in God and He comes through everyday. The little testimonies, the little improvements, the first words, the first glance, the first point of the finger, the first kick of the ball, or the first snap of a button - these are all milestones for us as parents and we celebrate them together and praise God for His mercies.

The move to high school started as a rocky road but our experience at ETHS was phenomenal. God blessed Yinka with 2 Angels that were his teachers for 4 years and under their care, he blossomed into a self-assured young man. He had played in the middle school band with the help and support of his lifelong music teacher. When he transitioned to high school, we decided to enroll him in the school band.

This was met with resistance as the schedule was too rigid to accommodate Yinka's needs. We were met with several arguments as to why he could not do band. It meant he would miss some academic learning. At this point, we were prepared to sacrifice the hope of Yinka being a scholar for the possibility of making him a musician if that was where his passion and talent lies. I encourage parents to find their child(ren)'s passion and focus on it. Every child has a unique gift, even children with special needs and it is important to hone in on those gifts and develop them so that your child can have a chance at something special that is unique to him. We decided to give up math instruction so that Yinka could walk half a mile within the school hall to the band room every 4th period. The teachers felt he could not find his way around a school of about three thousand students, but he did for 4 years and he had an aid initially walk him there. Sometimes his private music teacher would go and sit with him during the sessions to help him concentrate and catch up with the demands of the band room .

12: The Final Pieces of the Puzzle; Flight to the Future

When I started this book, my thought process was in pity mode and hence the title, "NO! NOT MY SON".

At this point in my journey, I can now look back and say, "Why not my son?" For many years I wondered why this should happen to me. I wondered what I had done wrong. I wondered if God had singled me out to punish me and make a public spectacle of me. Was there something I did wrong? I would think of all the sins I committed and wonder which one God was punishing me for.

Recently, a mother sat in my office in Lagos and as we talked about her child and the things she has been through, I realized they were the exact fears that I had but had never shared with another soul. I instantly felt a connection to her and her drive and determination reminded me so much of myself. She refused to take the life sentence that was passed on her son and later that week when I watched her with her son, I realized that God only chooses the strongest women on this earth to bless them with these unique children.

Every mother of a child with autism has an inner strength that radiates through. I embarked on a journey to save the children in my own diaspora.

I had worried about them for so long and thought who was there for them. It was a real struggle for me, and my life had changed so much. I was far from the young naive 25 year old that landed in JFK, ready to go and conquer God's own country. I decided that I must go and tell my people about everything that has happened to me and my family. I came to America with huge dreams and hopes that were accomplished but I got much more. God gave me much more than I could ever anticipate. God has trusted us with a special gift that I had not anticipated and could not have imagined. They must listen and know what it is like to overcome autism, so they too can have hope that having a child with a disability is not a life-long sentence but a world of possibilities, depending on what they make of it. You can let it break you or mold you into a rock that other people can step on, so they do not have to sink while navigating this maze of Autism Spectrum Disorder.

I was ecstatic to find out that God had sent some angels ahead of me. I met Dr. Yinka Akindayomi, who gave me hope and encouraged me. She was a pediatrician who returned from England with her son, who was on the autism spectrum. When she could not find services for her young son, she decided to create her own. This inspired me.

In 2007, I founded the Braintech International Resource Center (BIRC) in Lagos which was a center for brain fitness. Our mission was to promote brain fitness through behavioral technology.

I was inspired to start Braintech International Resource Center (BIRC) – a center for brain fitness.

The center was committed to increasing the quality of life of individuals living with various disabilities that limit their overall executive functioning.

After a bitter experience with expatriates we had partnered with to start Braintech, I returned to the United States and enrolled in a Masters Program for Clinical Psychology in 2009. The experience was a grueling one but the support of my family and friends around me kept me going. The decision to return to school was born out of the helplessness I felt when greed overtook the people I had invited to join in the journey to help my kinsmen. If this was to be done, I could not depend on "experts" who looked to exploit desperate families and were all about the profit and not the altruistic humanitarian venture that we had embarked on. I swore never to be stranded in this journey and never to be at the mercy of any "professional". I completed my Masters in Clinical Psychology in 2011 and my professors encouraged me to go for the doctoral program. They explained that this would allow me to work independently and have a global presence. In September 2016, I graduated with a Doctorate Degree in Clinical Psychology. After I completed my program, I worked with a Medical Clinic as a resident psychologist. I spend my time these days helping other families navigate the maze of autism. I speak to young mothers receiving the diagnosis for the first time. I work with families going through what I call the stages of grief as it relates to autism. All I can do is offer help, support, guidance and a soft landing so they do not have to struggle getting through the maze.

2018 Updates

This month, the 25th of December to be precise, Yinka will be 21 years Old. This is a big deal for our family. It is a milestone age for him. God has been indeed good to us. He has seen my family and I through many turbulent events but to the glory of God we are still standing. We are still here and all the glory belongs to him. He asked to spend his birthday in Disneyworld and since this is the first time he would make a request about his birthday, it was Disneyworld.

After he graduated from high school, Trinity University band offered him an opportunity to play alongside their students during their basketball games. Recently, Yinka started to play with the church band and he loves every moment of it. It gives me so much joy watching him play the trombone with such joy and satisfaction. He also joined a community band, The New Horizon Band at the Music Institute of Chicago, where he is currently the only trombonist on the band.

2019 Updates

My Oldest son graduated from college and my youngest turns 18 in a few months and will be off to college in the fall of 2021.

I now run a Therapy and Diagnostic center in Lagos, where I am able to help people on a larger scale. Our center Therapeutic Solutions works not only with children on the spectrum, but those who have a variety of diagnosis. We also offer Therapy services to adults as well as administer psychological assessments.

God has been good to me and I have nothing but praises and thanksgiving to him. Today, I enjoy speaking about mental health in various communities. I also counsel and mentor other parents who are going through the same journey I went through.

2020 Updates

Yinka will be 23 this year and he is still a work in progress. He is a talented musician and plays the piano as well as the trombone. He is very organized and meticulous in his everyday life and as long as he has a routine he can follow, he is fine. The 2020 lock down due to COVID-19 has been challenging but we were able to find some virtual programs for him that he enjoys and looks forward to. I was also able to take the time to finally complete this book and for that I am grateful.

This is my life story and I am proud to share my experiences with another whose journey may just be starting.

Pictures

ABOUT THE AUTHOR

Dr. Tade Akere started to write this book many years ago after her middle son was diagnosed with Autism. This diagnosis led her to pursue a Doctorate degree in Clinical Psychology. Her personal and professional experience with Autism has made her a mentor and consultant to many families across the globe.

She is the founder of Braintech International Resource center (BIRC), a non-profit organization that provides screening, consultations and support for families of individuals with autism and other disabilities. An arm of BIRC is the Michaels' Army that meets once a month to pray for children and individuals with Autism and other disabilities.

Dr. Akere is also the Clinical Director at Therapeutic Solutions located in Lagos, Nigeria and the Director of Administration with Raphael Medical Services in Chicago, Illinois.

She is married to Dr. Ayoade Akere and they are blessed with three amazing sons - Ayodeji, Ayoyinka and Ayokitan.